THE BIG BOOK OF DOGS

THE BIG BOOK OF

Text by FELIX SUTTON • Pictures by PERCY LEASON

DOGS

GROSSET & DUNLAP • NEW YORK • Publishers

COPYRIGHT, 1952, BY GROSSET & DUNLAP, INC. LITHOGRAPHED IN THE UNITED STATES OF AMERICA
ISBN: 0-448-00320-1 (Trade Edition)
ISBN: 0-448-03674-6 (Library Edition)
1976 PRINTING

THE ST. BERNARD has been the hero of many stories of bravery and courage. For almost 300 years, this intelligent dog has been famous for his rescue work among travelers lost in the deep snows and paralyzing cold of the Swiss Alps. The St. Bernard was originally owned and trained by the monks of the Hospice of St. Bernard, a monastery situated high in a dangerous Alpine pass. After a heavy snowfall, the dogs would go out in teams of three or four to search for people who might have become stranded in the drifts. When they found a lost traveler, one or two of the dogs would lie down beside him to warm him with their body-heat, and lick his face to bring him back to consciousness. The others, meanwhile, hurried back to the hospice to bring

human help. Each dog carried a flask of brandy hung around his neck to help the victim revive himself. In this way, St. Bernards have saved between 2,500 and 3,000 lives. While travel through the Alps is not as dangerous today as it used to be, hardly a winter goes by that some snowbound traveler is not saved from freezing to death by the great dogs. The St. Bernard is a tall and very heavy dog. He has a massive head, powerful shoulders, big feet and a broad, bushy tail. Yet in spite of his extreme size, he makes a wonderful household pet. He is gentle, affectionate, quick to learn. And he is especially good as a companion and watchful guardian for small children.

Irish Setter

Wire-haired Pointing Griffon

Curly-coated Retriever

Field Spaniel

Cocker Spaniel

THE SPORTING DOG was bred to hunt game birds and wild waterfowl. Pointers, Setters and Spaniels are trained to find upland game birds, such as quail, partridge, woodcock and pheasant. Retrievers are used to swim out into the water and bring back ducks and geese that have been shot down by hunters.

The Sporting Dog was first developed in the British Isles during the Middle Ages. He was originally used to retrieve

Chesapeake Bay Retriever

Brittany Spaniel

Gordon Setter

Weimaraner

American Water Spaniel

Irish Water Spaniel

game that had been killed by falcons. The Spaniel—or, as he was then called, the "Spanyell"—was the first of the Sporting Dogs. Almost all of the other Sporting breeds are his descendants.

The real development of the Sporting Dog came after the invention of gunpowder, when game birds were hunted with fowling pieces, or shotguns, rather than with bows and arrows.

Clumber Spaniel

Labrador Retriever

German Short-haired Pointer

THE POINTER is a strong, clean-limbed, smooth-haired gun dog. He is a great favorite with hunters because of his speed, alertness and accuracy in finding quail, pheasant, partridge and other game birds. The Pointer hunts by running rapidly back and forth across the hunting field. When his keen sense of smell locates a bird, he "freezes"—holds his body rigid and "points" his nose in the direction of the place where the bird is hiding motionless in the grass.

THE GOLDEN RETRIEVER is one of the most beautiful of all gun dogs. His job is to swim out and retrieve ducks and other waterfowl after his master has shot them down. The Golden Retriever is easy—and fun—to train. He loves to chase sticks and balls when they are thrown for him. And he is a natural water dog. The Golden Retriever is growing more popular every day, not only as a duck-hunter's helper, but as a children's pet as well.

THE ENGLISH SETTER is also a hunting dog. He is built very much like the Pointer except that his coat is long. Like the Pointer, he, too, points his game. He got his name, however, because 300 to 400 years ago in England he was trained to crouch down and "sit" on his haunches when he found a bird. The Setter is a beautiful and intelligent dog, and his pleasant disposition makes him an ideal household pet.

THE ENGLISH SPRINGER SPANIEL is more popular today as a house pet than as a gun dog, although he was originally bred for hunting. Unlike the Pointer and the Setter, he does not point his birds. Instead, he pounces in upon them, and makes them fly into the air so that his master can get a shot at them. The Springer in this picture has retrieved a Ring-neck Pheasant, one of our best-known game birds.

Afghan Hound

Otterhound

Basset Hound

THE HOUND is a hunting dog—and was probably the first type of dog to be domesticated by early man. In prehistoric days, dogs were wild, wolflike animals that lived by running down and killing game. The ancient peoples tamed dogs so they could train them to help hunt the animals on which man depended for food

Greyhound and Whippet

Basenji

Norwegian Elkhound

Wolfhound

Black-and-Tan Coonhound

Borzoi

Beagle

and clothing. As the centuries went by, the various breeds of Hound were developed, each for his ability to hunt a particular kind of animal.

Hounds differ from Sporting Dogs (bird dogs) in that they hunt by following a scent on the ground, while the Sporting Dog follows a scent in the air.

Harrier

Saluki

Deerhound

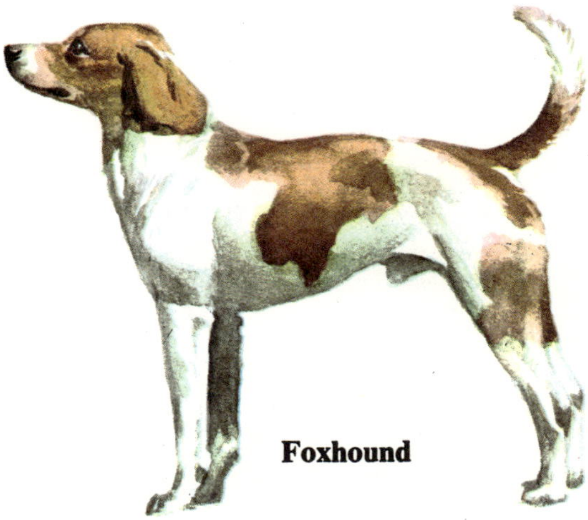

Foxhound

Newfoundland

Samoyede

Old English Sheep Dog

Rottweiler

Pulik

WORKING DOGS do just what their name implies. They work for their living. Usually they are employed as herd dogs or draft animals.

Dogs of the Working group have tremendous strength, unusual powers of endurance and a high order of intelligence. With few exceptions, they are loyal companions, devoted to their masters.

Great Pyrenees

Belgian Sheep Dog

Siberian Husky

Bernese Mountain Dog

Kuvasz

Australian Kelpie

Welsh Corgi

Except for the Welsh Corgi and the Belgian Sheep Dog, the dogs pictured on this page are not often kept as family pets. But the farmer, the sheepherder, the trapper, the policeman—and all the other people who have come to rely on the help of the Working Dog—will tell you he is the staunchest friend and companion that any man ever had.

Alaskan Malemute

Komondor

THE PARTS OF YOUR DOG

The dog shown here is a Great Dane. But the names of the parts of his body are common to all dogs. In an official American Kennel Club Dog Show, a dog is judged by the excellence of his various features. If you love dogs and want to know more about them, you should memorize this chart. Practice pointing out the parts of your own dog until you know their names by heart.

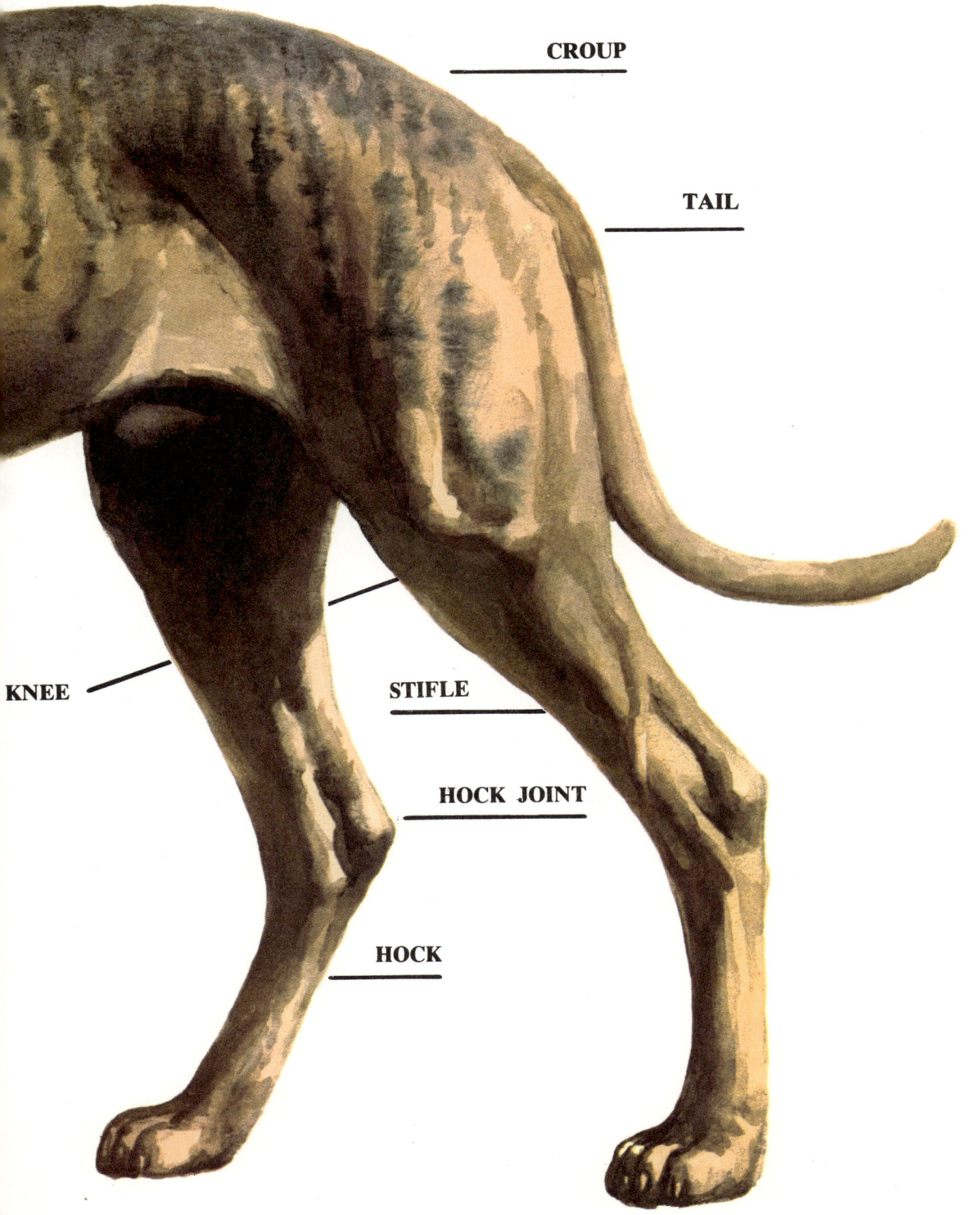

THE ESKIMO DOG is the "work horse" of the frozen, snow-covered lands in the Far North. During most of the year, the Eskimo dog provides the only means of transportation for the Alaskan natives and the white hunters and trappers. He is not an especially big dog, when compared to the St. Bernard. But he is probably the toughest and strongest dog of his size in the world. Hitched to a sled, in teams of seven, nine or eleven dogs, he can pull heavier loads over greater distances than almost any other work animal. Eskimo dog teams have hauled heavily loaded sleds as far as 100 miles in a single day. The Eskimo dog is also an excellent and fearless hunter. His sensitive nose can find seals that are hidden under the ice, and he will not hesitate to

attack an animal as big as a polar bear. The typical Eskimo dog has a thick neck, a wolflike muzzle, slanting eyes, erect ears and a powerfully muscled body. He is protected from the severe cold by an extremely thick and luxuriant coat, and his feet are broad and heavily padded for easy traveling over the snow. Temperatures as low as 40 to 50 degrees below zero do not bother him at all. At night, he simply curls up in a snowdrift, tucks his nose under his tail for warmth and sleeps snugly until morning. He stays strong and healthy on a diet of raw fat, and walrus or seal meat. Eskimo dogs are not often kept as household pets, although many of them are friendly and affectionate. In this country they are used mostly for dog racing.

Sealyham

Bedlington

Manchester

Wire-haired and Smooth Fox Terriers

THE TERRIER was originally a hunting dog who dug into the ground after such burrowing animals as woodchucks, foxes, gophers and badgers. His name comes from the Latin word *terra*, meaning earth. Today, not many Terriers are used for hunting. As a class, they are probably the most popular of all household pets.

Terriers are friendly, alert and intelli-

Skye

Airedale

Cairn

Irish

Bull Terrier

Scottish and Dandie Dinmont

Schnauzer

gent. They learn quickly. They are active, hardworking, and have boundless energy. They are extremely courageous. In a fight, a Terrier will stand up to a dog many times his size.

The Terrier is an excellent watchdog, a faithful and considerate playmate for children. And he thinks that his master is the most wonderful person in the world.

West Highland White

Welsh

Kerry Blue

DOGS WITH A JOB TO DO • The dog has always been a faithful friend, a loyal companion and a hard-working servant to man. But some dogs deserve very special recognition for the outstanding services they perform.

WAR DOGS *(upper left)* better known as the K-9 Corps, were used in World War II by the Army, the Navy, the Marines and the Coast Guard. They worked as sentries, scouts and first-aid assistants—and several were decorated with our country's highest awards for bravery.

BLOODHOUNDS *(upper right)* have the most highly developed sense of smell of any dogs. For this reason, they are widely used to track down escaped criminals. The Bloodhound's nose is so accurate that his "evidence" has often been accepted in a court of law.

CIRCUS DOGS *(middle left)* are the most versatile of all performing animals—and the most

appealing. The Circus Dog is usually a Terrier or a Poodle. The trainer and the dogs spend months perfecting tricks which entertain their audiences.

SEEING EYE DOGS (*middle right*) perform one of the finest services of all—that of leading blind people safely through city streets. These dogs require long periods of training, but when they have learned their duties they work with almost human intelligence.

CART DOGS (*lower left*) have been used for centuries as draft animals in the Low Countries of Europe—particularly Belgium and Holland. It is common, even today, to see these sturdy dogs hauling cartloads of farm produce into the city.

THE SHEPHERD DOG (*lower right*) is one of man's most trusted helpers. He maintains an alert watch over his flock. If one of his charges strays away, he quickly brings it back to safety.

Pomeranian

Mexican Hairless

Chihuahua

Pug

Pekingese

Pinscher (Miniature)

THE TOY DOG, unlike the Hound, the Sporting Dog, the Working Dog and the Terrier, was bred to serve no other purpose than to be a fine family pet. Toys are small—the Chihuahua often weighs less than a pound—and so they are admirably suited to their job.

Most Toys are dwarf specimens of larger breeds—such as the English Toy Spaniel, the Italian Greyhound, the Pug and the Toy Poodle. But, tiny as they are, Toys are excellent watchdogs. You often read stories in the newspapers about Toys who have aroused their families and saved them when the house was on fire.

The Pekingese is probably the oldest of the Toy Dogs.

Bull-Mastiff

Chow

Schipperke

Bulldog

Keeshond

COMPANION, GUARD AND OTHER DOGS • The dogs pictured on these two pages do many different kinds of work. The Bulldog and the Mastiff were bred in early England as fighting dogs. The Bull-Mastiff, a cross between them, was first developed as a watchdog to keep poachers out of game preserves. The Schipperke and the Keeshond are also widely used as guard dogs.

The Redbone and the English Fox-

Redbone Hound

Poodle

Boxer

Mastiff

Boston Terrier

Dachshund

hound are used for hunting in our Southern states. The Bouvier des Flandres is a farm dog, who seems to take naturally to cattle driving. The Chow, the Boxer, the Boston Terrier, the Dachshund and the Poodle all make fine friends and good companions.

And who hasn't seen a Dalmatian, the favorite pet of firemen, perched on the front seat of a fire engine as it dashes through the streets to answer an alarm?

Dalmatian

Bouvier des Flandres

English Foxhound

CHOOSING YOUR DOG • If you love dogs, almost any puppy can win your heart the first time you see him. However, you and your dog will be together for a long time and you will want to be completely happy with each other. Therefore, you should choose your dog with care. For example, if you live in the country or in a small town, you may want one of the larger breeds—a Boxer, a Setter or a Shepherd. Remember that big dogs need plenty of room to run. If you live in a city apartment, you will probably be better off with a Cocker, a Dachshund, a Terrier or one of the other smaller breeds who are content to live mostly indoors.

The best time to buy a puppy is when he is about two months old. Then you can train him exactly the way you want him trained, and you will not have to break him of any bad habits that he may have acquired. When choosing your puppy, pick out one that is active and alert. See how interested he is in what is going on around him and how quickly he responds when you speak to him. Take him off by himself, away from his brothers and sisters, and see how friendly and self-confident he seems. If he appears to be too timid or shy, you had better forget him and choose another puppy.

Look for a puppy who appears to be healthy and happy, who shows no signs of lameness or malformation, and who has good bones, good muscles and a good coat. Most important, buy your puppy from a reliable breeder. He loves dogs or he wouldn't be in the business.

Important: Very few dogs are able to understand words of more than one syllable. So give your puppy a *short* name, one that he can recognize instantly.

HOW TO TRAIN YOUR PUPPY

Your dog's behavior, in and out of the house, depends upon what you teach him. Everything he will know about living happily with people, he must learn from *you*. Most dogs are naturally intelligent. If you are patient with your dog, he will learn quickly. If you are not, he will become confused. Don't rush your puppy's training. Teach him *one* thing at a time and work with him until he has learned it thoroughly, before going on to something else.

Your Dog's Bed • The first thing you should provide for your puppy is a good bed. It needn't be fancy. A box, lined with old blankets or an old cushion, will do. Always keep it clean.

Housebreaking Your Puppy • Housebreaking is the first, and most important, part of your puppy's education. Begin training him the first day you have him at home. Start out with a regular routine. Feed your puppy at the same time every day so he will form the habit of eliminating regularly. After his feeding, take him out on a leash or, if there is no traffic, put him outdoors for a run by himself. Give your puppy a run the first thing in the morning, the last thing at night, and several times during the day. Before long he will get the idea and will ask to go out, by whining and scratching at the door.

If you live in an apartment or where it is difficult to take your puppy outdoors, teach him to use a box filled with torn newspapers. Put him into the box a short time after he has eaten and make him stay there until he has done what is expected of him. Change the paper in the box every day, but *always leave in a few soiled pieces*. Don't forget that a dog remembers with his nose!

If your puppy misbehaves in the house, don't punish him until you catch him in the act. Otherwise, he probably won't know what he is being punished for, and will become confused. When you do catch him misbehaving, spank him *on the spot* with a folded newspaper. Tell him sharply, *"No! No! No!"* and put him outdoors or into his box. When you clean up his mistake, use a strong-smelling disinfectant. This will discourage him from revisiting the same spot.

Caution: Don't give a puppy too much water. Let him drink only after meals or when he begs for it.

Teaching Your Dog to Come When You Call • When your puppy runs away from you, as he often will until he is well trained, never shout at him and never, *never* run toward him. He knows that he can outrun you and he will think you are playing a game. Instead, kneel down on the ground, hold out your hand, whistle and call to him in a friendly tone of voice. He will find this kind of attention very hard to resist. When he finally comes to you, pat him and reward him with a bit of food. He will soon associate his coming to you with a reward—and he will come every time you call.

Teaching Your Dog to Sit • It is easy to teach your dog to sit on command. Call him to you, slip his leash over his head and say, "Sit!" As you repeat the word, hold his head up with the leash and press down on his rump. As soon as he is in the sitting position, give him a bit of food as a reward and pat him to show that you think he is a good dog. Make him remain sitting until you say, "Up!" or "O.K.!" and then let him up. Repeat this over and over until he understands what you want him to do.

Teaching Your Dog to Lie Down • After your dog has learned to sit at command, you can teach him to lie down. First, order him to sit. Then put his leash around his neck, pull downward on it and say, "Down!" As you repeat the word, push him to the ground by pressing on his shoulders. When he obeys, give him a reward and pat him. Keep him in the down position until you tell him, "Up!" or "O.K.!" Repeat the lesson patiently until he has thoroughly learned it.

Teaching Your Dog to Walk on a Leash • When you are walking your dog on a leash, it is natural for him to become so interested in all the things around him that he pulls, tugs, turns around and sometimes gets his leash all tangled up with your legs. Here is an easy way to teach him to walk along quietly by your side: In the same hand in which you are holding the leash, carry a piece of dog biscuit or some other tidbit. When your dog sees and smells that you have something good for him to eat, he will follow along with his eyes and nose exactly as you want him to do. After a few minutes, give him the tidbit. Soon you will find that walking quietly along by your side on a loose leash will become a habit with him.

Feeding Your Dog • What you should feed your dog depends upon his age, his breed and his size. Most authorities agree that one-half to two-thirds of every meal for a grown dog should be lean meat. The remainder can be scraps from the family table. Most commercial dog foods are good, and they are easy to prepare.

Give your dog plenty of *big* bones to gnaw on between meals. This keeps his teeth and gums in good condition. But always make sure they are *big* bones. Never give him chicken, lamb or fish bones!

Don't give your dog fat meat, fish, potatoes or beans. *Never* give him pork.

The safest thing is not to try to decide your dog's diet for yourself. Ask your veterinarian, or the breeder from whom you bought him, and then follow his advice!

Keeping Your Dog Healthy • The most common ailment that pesters a puppy is *worms*. These are the symptoms to look for: If your pup is always hungry—or if, on the other hand, he has no appetite—if his stomach is bloated—if he looks too thin or scrawny—if his coat is dull and dry—if he seems listless and spiritless—then the chances are that he has worms. You should take him to a good veterinarian at once. Even if your puppy shows no outward signs of worms, he probably has a mild case of them anyway. Most puppies do. Therefore he should be wormed when he is two months old, and again every four or five weeks until he is five or six months old. Your veterinarian will suggest a good worm medicine.

Distemper is one of the most serious dog diseases, and also one of the most common. It is frequently fatal and almost always leaves bad aftereffects. Every puppy should be inoculated against distemper when he is two months old. When you buy your puppy, ask if he has been inoculated with anti-distemper serum. If he has not, take him to a veterinarian and have it done.

Many of the symptoms of distemper are the same as those listed here for worms. So here is a good rule to remember: Whenever your puppy looks and acts sick, don't try to doctor him yourself. Take him to a veterinarian!

A Few Good Things to Know • Dogs should not be washed too often. Instead, give your dog a brisk brushing with a good, *stiff* brush every day. This will help to keep his skin healthy, it will discourage fleas, and will keep his coat bright, clean and shining.

Never hit a dog with your hand! When you have to punish him, use a folded newspaper or the end of his leash. Remember that your hands are for patting and praising, to tell your dog you like him.